My Bible Dress-Up Book

Carla Williams

A Faith Parenting Guide can
be found on page 64.

Dedicated to:
my sons and to the many, many children who have come and gone from our
home over the past twenty five years. Thank you for teaching me how to
become childlike (Matthew 18:4).

A special thanks to my editor and friend, Jeannie Harmon,
for all the many frustrating hours she spent on this book.
Carla Williams

Faith Kids™ is an imprint of
Cook Communications Ministries, Colorado Springs, CO 80918
Cook Communications, Paris, Ontario
Kingsway Communications, Eastbourne, England

MY BIBLE DRESS-UP BOOK
© 2000 by Carla Williams for text.

Edited by Jeannie Harmon
Designed by Helen Harrison—YaYe Design
Photographer: Gaylon Wayne Wampler
Illustrations by Victoria Hummel
Models: Matthew Tortorich, Geo Surrat, Anthony Kaufman, Carley Kocel,
    and Alexa Liddie

First printing, 2000
Printed in Canada
04 30 02 01 00   5 4 3 2 1

ISBN 0-78143-436-X

Table of Contents

Introduction

Can you imagine sailing a huge boat full of animals or parting a sea or fighting a giant? Think of what it would be like to spend the night in the den of lions. If you like reading the wonderful true stories in the Bible, why not dress up and pretend to be your favorite Bible hero? Maybe you can put on a skit for Mom and Dad. They may even want to pull out the video camera and film you so you can watch yourself later. Invite some friends and put on a complete play!

On the pages that follow, we will give you instructions for putting together all kinds of neat costumes. Most of the items you need could be right there in your house. Dig into your closet or ask Mom or Dad if they have the items you need. You'll be surprised at treasures you'll find for making the perfect Bible costume. Be sure to check with a grown-up to make sure it is alright to use what you find.

Take a trip to the local thrift store or stop at the garage sale on the corner. We bet you'll find lots of neat stuff to add to your collection. Here's a shopping list of things to look for:

- **Shawls, ties, and scarves**
- **Belts and chains**
- **Lace curtains and tablecloths**
- **Beads, jewelry, brooches, etc.**
- **Robes and skirts**
- **Feathers and ribbons**
- **Funny sandals and big boots**
- **Fuzzy blankets and old towels**

- **Old sheets and pillow cases**
- **Lots of ribbons, belts, cords, etc.**
- **Cotton batting**
- **Poster board, construction paper, tissue paper**
- **Big boxes and little boxes**
- **Big safety pins, masking tape, and fabric glue**

How to Use This Book

The first part of the book gives instructions on how to make a simple tunic that you can wear with all the Bible costumes. Each story gives ideas for adding to the basic tunic to make it look like a specific Bible character.

Each story unit in this book appears on four pages. On the first two pages of each unit, you'll find a picture of a completed costume and instructions on how to dress up like that particular Bible character. On the third page, you will find a brief Bible story and a reference telling you where to find this story in your Bible. On the fourth page, you'll find instructions for adding scenery and props if you decide to put on a play. Also, look for these special features:

- ● Think about This—questions to get you thinking about the story
- ● Collecting Details—interesting facts about the character or story
- ● Comedy Act—a joke or short funny story
- ● From the Script—a Bible verse to help you understand the story better

In the back of the book are ideas for more costumes and suggestions for writing plays. And on the very last page of the book are some ideas for Mom and Dad to join in the fun.

Before You Begin

- ● Check with an adult before dragging everything out. It takes time to put together some of the costumes. Make sure you have enough time to get dressed up and still play.
- ● Carefully read the instructions and gather together everything you need first. Maybe you can substitute pieces if you don't have exactly what is suggested.
- ● You may need help from an adult to make the costumes, so ask before you start.
- ● You might want to read the Bible story or even look up the story in the Bible so you are familiar with the Bible character.
- ● If you are putting on a play, take some time to write the skit using the suggestions in Get Ready, Set, Action! on pages 62 and 63.

When You Have Finished

- ● Find an old suitcase, chest, or box to store your tunic and costume pieces.
- ● Return anything you borrowed from someone else.
- ● Clean up your props and scenery.
- ● If an adult videotaped you, sit down and watch the show!

The Tunic

In Bible times, tunics were used as undergarments, so the tunic is the basis for every costume in this book. For some of the characters, the tunic will be the main costume. For others, it will be worn under a cloak or robe. Some costumes will call for a long tunic and others will need you to have a short tunic. You can wear it with or without a belt, but a belt will help you adjust the fit. The tunic can be easily slipped over your head.

Tunic Material

Tunics should be made out of light-weight, stretchable fabric. Dark colors such as browns and blues go with every costume, but you can choose whatever color you like best to make your tunic.

A Tunic's Width

You want to make the tunic your size. To do this, measure from the end of one shoulder, across your chest, to the end of your other shoulder. See Choosing Material.

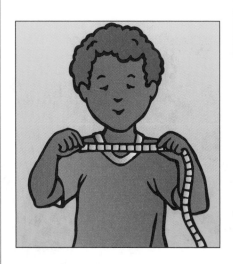

Tunic Length

The length of your tunic will depend on whether your Bible character needs a long tunic or a short tunic to complete the costume. A long tunic will go to your ankles and a short one will go to your knees. You can make your tunic a little in between and adjust it with a belt to the desired length. Whatever you decide, you will need to cut the width of your tunic

first. Once the width is cut, you should fold the cloth in half and hold it against your body. Tuck the fold under your chin. With the material under your chin, ask someone to help you to mark where you want the length to be. From this mark, you will know where to cut. If you plan to wear a belt, cut the fabric a little longer, because you will pull the tunic up when you wear a belt.

You can also measure the length with a tape measure. Hold one end of your measuring tape at your shoulder. Have a helper pull down

Choosing Material

Most material with a little stretch is going to be 60 inches in width at fabric stores. The names of these fabrics are knits, double-knits, robe material, or T-shirt knit. Because the fabric is so wide, you can make two tunics out of one length of material. You will not need to measure your shoulders if you use 60-inch material. To do this, cut on the fold line from the store to divide the material in half. It will take about 1-3/8 to 2-3/4 yards of material, depending on your size. Decide which tunic length your tunic needs to be before you start cutting. See Tunic Length.

the tape so that it hangs straight down from your shoulder to your toes. Decide where you want the length and write the number of inches from your shoulder to the desired length. Double this number for the length of the material. To have a tunic for every Bible costume, you might want to make a long one and a short one. Remember, if you use 60-inch width fabric you can make two tunics—one long and one short.

Tunic Instructions

Make several tunics and ask some friends to join you in putting on a full production of the stories in this book.

1 Fold the cloth in half so that the fold is at the top. Hold it up against you to make sure it is the right length and wide enough from shoulder to shoulder.

2 Place the folded fabric on a flat surface, such as a table or floor. Remember the fold is the top of the tunic. Fold fabric in half again, but this time, widthwise so that it is long and thin.

3 The corner of the fabric that has no raw edges—only folds, is the corner where you will make your neck hole. Make a really **tight** fist. Place your fist on the corner and outline it with a pencil. Keep your fist tight as you draw a half circle for a neck hole.

4 Keeping the material folded, cut over the line you have drawn to cut the corner off. Cut it round or square it off.

5 Unfold the tunic and slip it over your head to make sure the hole is big enough. Trim it larger if needed.

6 Turn the material wrong side out and fold in half again with the head hole at the top. Making sure that you leave holes for arms, you can machine stitch or use fabric glue to close the sides. If you would rather not use fabric glue or stitch the sides closed, you can use a belt to keep the tunic in place.

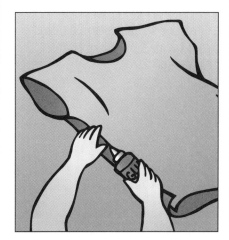

Now you're ready to add accessories—robes, shawls, and jewelry—to your tunic and pretend that you are your favorite Bible character! Each story will tell you what to do.

You will find additional ideas on pages 60 and 61.

Head Covering

The Bible characters in this book wore traditional head cloths much like those of wandering Arab tribes. Today in the Middle East, many still wear a similar head cloth. Here's how to make your own:

1 Ask Mom for an old pillowcase, scrap material, dish towel, or bath towel.

2 Place it on your head.

3 Hold the cloth in place by tying a cord or cloth belt around your forehead.

Shoes

Dig out your summer sandals. For most characters you will want to wear sandals. But for some you may want to go barefoot.

Snowboots work great for soldiers.

Noah

Casting Call All the world had become wicked. God needed a man who was righteous and blameless for an important job. Obedience was what God wanted, and Noah was the perfect man for the part. The Bible tells us that Noah did everything God told him to do.

Wardrobe

For the Noah costume, you'll need Mom or Dad's old bathrobe, a cloth belt or cord, masking tape or safety pins, yarn or string, cotton batting, and your favorite stuffed animals.

Collecting Details

Read the complete story of Noah in Genesis 6-9 to find the answers to the following questions.

Which bird told Noah that the water had dried up?

How many days were Noah and his family shut up in the ark?

Noah's Robe

1 Make a basic tunic following the directions on page 7. Then put the bathrobe over the tunic.

2 Measure how long your robe should be so that it doesn't drag on the floor. Mark it with masking tape.

3 Take off the robe. At the line you marked, fold the bottom of the robe up on the right side. Using safety pins about four inches apart, pin the robe to keep the hem in place. This will form pouches around the outside of the robe. If you don't want to use safety pins, use

masking tape, but fold the robe to the inside so that the tape is hidden.

4 Stick small stuffed animals in the outside pouches so that the animals can be seen.

5 Put the robe back on and tie the belt. Stick stuffed animals in belt, pockets, and anywhere else you can find room. You can even pin a few on your shoulder if you like.

Noah's Beard

There are lots of ways to make beards and you will learn some of them throughout this book. Here is an easy way to give Noah a long white beard.

1 Cut a 12-inch square of cotton batting with scissors. This material is white, thick, and fuzzy, and can be found in any fabric department. Cotton batting is often used in making quilts.

2 Round the edges of one end of the batting.

3 Tie a 10-inch piece of string or yarn at each of the top corners. Tie it around your head. This will bunch up the batting a little so it makes the beard look fuller.

4 With a pencil, draw a small line where your mouth is located. Take off the beard and cut a mouth hole where you placed your mark.

Additional Props for Noah

- Carry a broomstick as a staff to herd animals.
- Lots and lots of stuffed animals. If you have pets, maybe they will cooperate with you to be part of your production.
- Put a hammer in one pocket for building the ark. Be careful not to hurt yourself or someone else with it.

Noah and the Great Flood

God was very sad. Almost all the people on the earth did evil things. God was tired of all the wickedness, so He decided to flood the whole earth. But there was one man who loved God and tried to please God with his actions. His name was Noah. God decided to save Noah and his family.

"Noah," said God. "I am going to make it rain. A great flood will cover the earth. Everyone will die. But I will save you and your family. I want you to build a big boat."

Noah obeyed God. He and his sons worked hard. They cut down trees and built a boat called an ark. They put tar on the bottom and sides so no water could leak into the boat. It took a long time to build the ark. Finally, they were finished. God was pleased.

"Now, Noah, gather two of every kind of animal," said God. "Put them on the ark with you and your family."

Again Noah obeyed God and gathered all the animals into the ark. Then Noah, his wife, and his three sons and their wives entered the ark. When everyone was inside, God shut the door. It began to rain. It rained and rained and rained. The ark began to float. The water rose higher and higher. It rained for forty days and nights. Soon the entire earth was covered with water. Then God stopped the rain.

All the people and animals on the earth were gone. But Noah, his family, and the animals on the ark were safe. It took many days and weeks for the water to go down. Noah and his family waited patiently inside the ark. When the ark rested on top of a mountain and the water dried up, Noah opened the door. His family and the animals ran out. They were so happy to touch dry ground again.

Noah told God, "Thank You, Lord, for saving us."

God was pleased with Noah. He promised never to flood the earth again. God put a rainbow in the sky to remind Noah and all of the people to come of His promise. God always keeps His promises.

—*Taken from Genesis 6–9*

Think
ABOUT
THIS

Imagine what it was like inside the ark. Do you think that the animals felt seasick?

How do you think Mrs. Noah felt?

What was the first thing Noah did when he left the ark? What would you have done first?

Setting the Scene

You will probably want to start your story with the scene of Noah building the ark. Then you can move Noah, his family, and the animals into the ark and have scene two inside the boat.

The Ark

1 Ask an adult if you can borrow a card table. Turn it on its side.

2 Hang a sheet over the legs to enclose the back of the table. If you don't have a card table, use the dining table or put several chairs together side by side.

3 Gather all your stuffed animals and put them under the sheet. Put on your Noah costume and pretend to be riding in the ark. Remember God's promise to Noah.

Teacher: Do you know who built the ark?

Student: No . . . uh.

Teacher: Correct.

Inside the Ark

If you are putting on a play about Noah, you will want to have a scene inside the ark. Gather pots, pans, baskets, and boxes to look like supplies in the ark. Surround the "stage" with stuffed animals. Think about how Noah and his family felt inside the big boat. What did it smell like? Do you think it was hot or cold? What were the sounds?

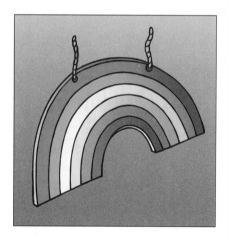

Special Effects

● Rattle a cookie sheet to sound like thunder.
● Flash the lights to look like lightning.
● You can draw a rainbow on poster board. Hang or tape it above the ark.
● Make animal sounds and record them into a tape recorder—roar like a lion, squawk like a bird, squeak like a mouse, or moo like a cow. Ask some friends to help you and make the sounds all together to sound like a lot of animals.

FROM THE
Script

By faith Noah, when warned about things not yet seen, in holy fear built an ark to save his family.

Hebrews 11:7

Joseph

Casting Call This story needed someone who could trust in God no matter what happened. Joseph got the part! He trusted God, even when his brothers betrayed him and sold him into slavery.

Wardrobe

You will need a basic tunic (see page 7), striped or multicolored material, a thin strip of material or cloth belt, and sandals.

Joseph's father made him a special coat of many colors. If you have a multicolored robe available, you can wear that over your tunic. Or you can make Joseph's coat by following the directions on page 13.

Collecting Details

Who had a dream about seven heads of grain being scorched by a hot wind from the east?
(Genesis 41:1–18)

Joseph had a younger brother. What was his name?
(Genesis 45:14)

Coat of Many Colors

1 Pick multicolored or striped material of the same type as your basic tunic.

2 Follow all the instructions on Pages 6 and 7 to make another tunic.

3 To make a coat, cut a straight line up the middle of the front of this tunic.

4 Now you have a coat to wear over your other tunic. You can trim the bottom to make it shorter than the other tunic if you want. Tie it with a belt or keep it open.

Joseph Costume

1 Put on your basic tunic.

2 Cover your tunic with the multi-colored robe.

3 Tie a strip of material around your head, like a headband.

Did you know they played tennis in ancient Egypt?

They must have, because Joseph served in Pharaoh's courts.

More Ideas:

- Add Joseph's brothers to the story by having some friends dress like shepherds as described on page 49.
- If you want to act out the story of Joseph in Egypt before Pharaoh, use the Egyptian costume on page 17. You can ask a friend to be Pharaoh.
- Joseph can wear the Egyptian costume when he becomes the governor of Egypt.

Additional Props:

- A broomstick for a shepherd's staff.
- Basket for Joseph to carry food to his brothers.

Joseph Goes to Egypt

Joseph was Jacob's favorite son. And even though Joseph had ten older brothers, Jacob gave Joseph a special gift.

"Joseph, I have something for you," Jacob said. "I made you this fine coat."

"Oh, Father, it is beautiful," Joseph said. "Thank you so much."

Joseph ran to show his brothers the special coat their father had given him. Jacob's older brothers were very jealous.

"Father never gave us such a nice coat," they all grumbled. They were angry and began to say bad things about Joseph.

One night Joseph had a dream. He told his brothers about his dream. "We were all working in the fields binding up bundles of grain. Suddenly, my bundle stood up and your bundles all bowed down to mine!"

"We will never bow down to you like a king," his brothers shouted. They hated him even more.

Soon Joseph had another dream. This time the sun and moon and eleven stars bowed down to Joseph.

"You think that even Father will bow down to you someday?" his brothers asked. "We will never bow down to you!"

One day while Joseph's brothers were in the hills tending sheep, Jacob said, "Go find out how your brothers are doing."

So Joseph set out to find his brothers. When Joseph's brothers saw him coming, they plotted to do something bad to him. They yanked off his beautiful coat and threw him into an old dry well.

Soon some traders came by on their way to Egypt. The brothers said, "Here's our chance to get rid of Joseph. Let's sell him as a slave!"

"No!" cried Joseph. But the brothers just laughed as they watched the men take Joseph and lead him away down the road to Egypt.

"What will we tell Father?" one brother asked.

"We will say a wild animal attacked Joseph!" another replied. The brothers tore Joseph's coat and stained it with goat's blood so that their father would believe their story. Jacob was very sad when he heard this news.

For many, many years Joseph was a slave in Egypt. He spent years in prison there as well. But God was faithful and watched over Joseph. God helped him to tell what people's dreams meant. Many people grew to like and respect Joseph.

One day Pharaoh had dreams that bothered him. He called Joseph to tell him what the dreams meant.

Joseph told Pharaoh, "Your dreams tell about seven years with plenty of food and water. Then there will be seven years of famine with no food. You must start preparing and saving up for those bad years."

Pharaoh liked Joseph's advice. "I will make you governor of all of Egypt!" said Pharaoh.

Joseph worked hard to prepare for the hard years when there would be no food. And when the bad years came, the famine spread to where Joseph's family lived. They grew very hungry.

"We hear that Egypt has plenty of food for everyone. We must go there to buy food so we won't die!" they cried. So Jacob sent his sons to Egypt to buy food.

When Jacob's sons arrived, they did not recognize the governor as their brother. Joseph revealed to them who he was. They were shocked and afraid because they feared that Joseph would want to get even with them for what they did to him. Instead, he forgave them and gave them lots of food. In the end, they did bow down to Joseph after all.

God had a plan to help the family of Jacob when they needed it most. God took care of Joseph while in Egypt. God takes care of those who trust in Him.

—*Taken from Genesis 37:1–36; 41:1–47*

Have you ever felt jealous of anyone?

How do you think Joseph felt toward his brothers when they sold him as a slave?

Setting the Scene

There are a lot of neat scenes in this story. You can start out in Jacob's tent, then move to the shepherd fields. Show Joseph in prison, then later in Pharaoh's court.

Sheep

Joseph's brothers were shepherds. You can make a sheep out of an old white pillow.

1 Shake or push down the inside stuffing from about five inches of one end of the pillow.

2 Use rubber bands to tie off each corner of the head end of the pillow to make floppy ears.

3 Tightly tie off 1/3 of the end with the ears to make the sheep's head.

4 Push and pull the stuffing to make the head pointed like a sheep's.

5 Use a black marker to color the backside of the ears. Color the inside pink.

6 Use a black marker to draw an eye on each side of the head.

7 Color a black snout starting halfway down the face and around to the bottom.

8 Fluff the bottom part of the pillow to make the sheep stand up. You may need to pin the back of the head to the body with a safety pin to keep the head from flopping over.

The Well

1 Make a circle using four kitchen style chairs, with the seats facing each other.

2 Wrap a dark blanket or sheet around the chairs, hiding them. Overlap the blanket into the inside of the circle.

3 Use masking tape to keep the blanket in place.

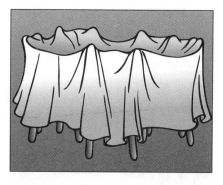

Joseph can hide in the well by scrunching down inside the circle of chairs.

More Ideas

- Hang dark blankets or sheets around the stage to look like a prison. Make paper chains for Joseph's hands and feet.
- Make a moon, sun, and eleven stars for Joseph's dream.
- Follow the instructions for Pharaoh's throne on page 19.

FROM THE
Script

Trust in the LORD with all your heart and lean not on your own understanding.

Proverbs 3:5

Moses and Pharaoh

Casting Call The Israelites had been in slavery for over 400 years. They needed someone who had enough faith in God to stand up to Pharaoh and lead the Israelites out of Egypt. God chose Moses. Although he was frightened at first, Moses put his faith in God to help him free God's people.

Wardrobe

Moses: You will need a basic tunic (see page 7), fake fur or bath towel, a new mop head, white felt, and poster board.

Pharoah: You will need your tunic (see page 7), 12" x 18" felt, craft jewels, empty bleach bottle, costume jewelry, a gold belt or chain, gold spray paint, cotton felt or batting, and craft glue.

Collecting Details

Check the references given to find the answers to the following questions.

What four creepy creatures did God send as plagues on the Egyptians?
              (Exodus 8—10:20)

What did God send to guide the Israelites at night as they left Egypt?   *(Exodus 13)*

Moses

1 Put on the basic tunic. Drape a piece of fake fur across your front from one shoulder to your waist. If you don't have fur, use an old bath towel or piece of material.

2 Make a head covering. (See Head Covering, page 7).

3 Make a white beard out of a mop head. (See instructions below.)

4 Hold a staff and carry two stone tablets cut from poster board or cardboard. If you want, write the Ten Commandments that God gave Moses on your tablets. Read Deuteronomy 5:6-21 to learn what they were.

Mop Beard

1 You will need a brand new string mop head. Cut the mop in half, loosening the strings.

2 Make another beard like the one you made for Noah, only use felt instead of batting. Make it shorter than Noah's beard. Don't forget to cut the mouth hole.

3 Glue the mop strings vertically onto the felt beard. Don't cover the mouth hole. Glue several layers

of strings to make a full beard. Hot glue works the best. MAKE SURE YOU HAVE ADULT SUPERVISION.

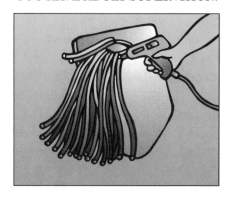

4 Cut smaller pieces of the mop to glue horizontally across the mustache area.

5 Tie the corners with string and tie around your head.

Pharaoh

1 Put on the basic tunic. A white tunic is the best for Pharaoh. If your tunic is another color, then you can drape a white sheet around your body. Use a gold belt or chain to hold up your tunic and sheet.

2 Put on the jeweled collar and hat. (See instructions.) Wear lots of jewelry, such as bracelets and chains. See page 60 to make a crown for Pharaoh.

Jeweled collar

1 Fold a 12" x 18" piece of felt in half so that the fold is 18" long and 6" wide.

2 Cut a half circle from one end to the other. (See illustrations.)

3 Keep the half circle folded. Find the center of the fold and mark

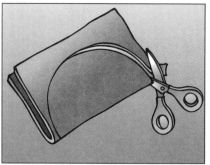

2 inches either side of the center. Now measure 2 inches down from the center and mark with a small dot. Draw a small half circle, between the two side marks, going through the dot.

4 Cut this half circle out of the center of the large half circle. It should look like a donut when you open it up.

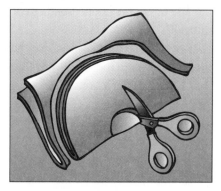

5 Fold the circle in half again. Start at one end and cut on the fold to the center circle. Cut only one end! Now the circle is a collar that fits around your neck.

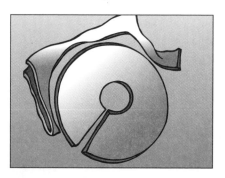

7 Glue on craft jewels or decorate with fabric paint.

17

Moses Goes Before Pharaoh

The Hebrews had been slaves in Egypt for over 400 years! Life was very hard for God's people. Pharaoh, who was the ruler in Egypt, made them work very hard in the hot sun. The Hebrews cried out to God to rescue them.

God watched over His people and decided to deliver them into a new land. God chose Moses to be their leader and with Moses' help, God would free the Hebrew people from bondage.

Moses went before Pharaoh. "Let my people go! God has promised to give them a new land!" Moses demanded.

"Ha! Who is this God! I don't know your God! We have our own gods in Egypt!" Pharaoh shouted. "Never will the Hebrews leave!"

Pharaoh was very angry. He made the people work even harder. Pharaoh forced them to make bricks out of straw, so he could build great buildings to honor himself.

But did that stop Moses? No, he just kept telling the people to trust God. "God wants us to leave Egypt. He has promised us a new land."

God said to Moses, "Go back to Pharaoh again. I will show him that I am God." So Moses kept on trying to talk to Pharaoh.

"Let my people go!" Moses said to Pharaoh.

"No! They will stay!" said the angry king.

Moses warned Pharaoh, "You will soon see the power of my God, the true God."

Pharaoh would not listen. Every time he said no, God sent a plague to the Egyptians. Bad things kept happening. First their water turned to blood. Then frogs hopped out of the rivers and filled all the Egyptian houses, including Pharaoh's! God sent thunder and lighting and hail that smashed and burned all the crops. Then huge clouds of locusts and flies came. Finally, God sent total darkness over Egypt. They couldn't see anything.

Every time Pharaoh would give in. "Moses, take your people and go! Your God is the true God," Pharaoh would say.

But then Pharaoh's heart would grow hard and he would change his mind. "No, you will never leave." And he grew angrier with every plague.

Then God told Moses, "I will send one more plague on Egypt. The oldest son in every family will die. Then Pharaoh will let My people go."

God told Moses some very important directions to follow. "Tell all the Hebrew people to mark their doors with the blood of a lamb. When I see that blood, I will pass over their house and not kill any Hebrew sons." So Moses told the people all that God had said.

God kept His promise and every thing happened just as He said. When Pharaoh's son died, he was very sad. He told Moses, "Go. Take the people and all of their herds and leave!"

Moses led God's people out of Egypt toward the promised land. They were free at last.

—*Taken from Exodus 5:1–11:10*

How do you think the Hebrews felt when they finally made it out of Egypt?

If you were a kid coming out of Egypt what would you take with you?

Setting the Scene

There are several scenes from the life of Moses that can be acted out. We have given you one story. Check out the Bible references below and see how many of the scenes you can create.

Baby Moses in the River

For your first scene, read Exodus 1:1-2:10. Pharaoh wanted to kill all the Hebrew baby boys. But God had a special plan for Moses. So Moses' mother put him in a basket and hid him in some reeds that grew on the river nearby.

1 Act out this scene by placing a doll inside a basket.

2 Put a blue sheet or blanket on the floor and scatter some plants on it. Place the basket on the sheet.

3 Use the queen costume on page 41 for Pharaoh's daughter.

Pharaoh's Throne

Make Pharaoh's throne by covering a chair with a sheet. Place a couple of plants on either side of the chair.

Who was the worst man in the Bible?

Moses, because he broke all the Ten Commandments at once (when he threw down the tablets)!

The Burning Bush

Read Exodus 3:1-4:17. God spoke to Moses through a burning bush. It was here that God told Moses to lead His people out of Egypt.

1 To make your own burning bush, tape strips of red and orange tissue paper onto a small, UNPLUGGED floor fan.

2 Plug it in and turn it on. The strips will blow to look like fire.

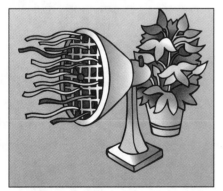

3 Put a plant behind it to look more like a bush.

The Red Sea

Read Exodus 13:17-14:31. After Pharaoh freed the Hebrews, his heart grew hard again. He ordered his army to chase the Hebrews. God saved the people by parting the Red Sea, allowing them to cross on dry land.

1 You can set this scene by spreading out a blue or green blanket or sheet on the floor.

2 Roll up some dark towels or sheets and set to one side. When you come to the part in the story where the people crossed over, roll the towels out on top of the blanket and cross through the Red Sea!

FROM THE
Script

The LORD is faithful to all his promises and loving toward all he has made.

Psalm 145:13b

Joshua

Casting Call Moses had died and God needed to choose a new leader for His people. He wanted someone who had courage to stand up to anyone who tried to keep the people from the land God had promised. Joshua fit the part. He knew God would help him to be strong and courageous.

Wardrobe

Joshua: The basic tunic (see page 7), a silver car windshield sun protector, ice cream tub, cardboard, aluminum foil, silver spray paint, shoe strings or string, a black or brown marker, and a thick belt.

CAUTION

Have adult supervision when using spray paint.

Armor

1 You will need to purchase a silver, shiny sun protector used for the car. Cut off the two end panels.

2 Tie these panels on the front of your legs with shoe strings or string.

3 Trim and round off the center remaining panel so that it looks like armor.

4 Pin the top edges to the back of your tunic with safety pins.

5 Wear a big belt around your waist to hold the rest of the armor close to your body.

Note: If you do not want to use a sun visor, you can make armor out of cardboard boxes. Cut it to the desired shape and size, and cover with aluminum foil.

Sword

1 Cut off one side of a large cardboard box. You can usually find one at the grocery store.

2 Draw the shape of a sword on the cardboard and carefully cut it out.

3 Wrap aluminum foil around the blade part of the sword. Color the handle with a black or brown marker.

Helmet

1 Paint a small plastic ice cream or sherbet tub with silver spray paint.

2 Cut two five-inch cardboard flaps that will go over your ears. Spray paint the flaps silver. Glue the flaps inside the helmet in the position of your ears.

Wear your winter boots, so you look like you are ready for battle.

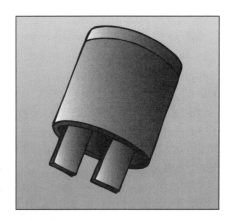

Shield

See page 29 for instructions.

Collecting Details

Who was saved in Jericho by a red thread?
(Joshua 2; Joshua 6:25)

What was Joshua's name before Moses changed it?
(Numbers 13:16)

Joshua and the Battle of Jericho

After Moses died, Joshua became the leader of the Hebrew people. God told Joshua, "Be strong and do not be afraid. I will help you lead the people to the promised land."

Joshua said to the people, "Get ready. We will soon cross the Jordan River into the new land God has given us."

God told Joshua, "Tell the priests to carry the ark of the covenant. They must cross the river first, then the people must follow after them."

The ark was a special box that held the tablets on which God wrote the Ten Commandments. It was covered with a layer of pure gold and was very beautiful. It usually sat in the tabernacle of God. No one could even touch it. The priests carried it with long poles that they slipped through rings on the side of the ark.

When the people saw the river, they were afraid. It was very high and at flood stage. But Joshua told the people, "Do not be afraid. God will help us cross the river."

As soon as the priests' feet touched the water, the river stopped flowing and dried up in front of them. The people crossed over on dry land to the promised land, called Canaan.

Unfortunately, those who were living in the new land didn't want to give it up to the Hebrews. The first city they came to was called Jericho. The king of Jericho didn't want to give his city to the Hebrews.

"We will fight them if they try to take our city," he told his people.

But God told Joshua, "I will give you this land, including the city of Jericho. Do not be afraid. I will give you a plan." So God told Joshua His plan to win against the army of Jericho.

Joshua shared the plan with the people. "We must march around the walls of the city once each day for six days. Do not say a word. Four priests will carry the ark. Seven other priests will blow horns. We will post armed guards in front and behind the ark. On the seventh day, march around the city seven times and when you hear the blast of the trumpets, shout to the Lord."

The people obeyed God's plan. They marched around Jericho for six days. Every day they walked around the city wall one time, then returned to their camp.

On the seventh day, the people marched around the city seven times. Can you imagine what the people inside the city thought? The last time around the wall, the priests blew their trumpets.

Joshua commanded the people, "Shout! The Lord has given us the city."

When they shouted, the walls fell down. The city of Jericho was in shambles. The Hebrew people ran into the city and took it from their enemies. God had a plan so that His people would win the battle. The people obeyed God and won!

—Taken from Joshua 1:3–6

Think ABOUT THIS

What do you think the people of Jericho said to each other as the Israelites marched around their city?

Why do you think it was important for the priests to carry the ark across the Jordan before the people crossed?

Setting the Scene

Joshua led an exciting life. There are many scenes that you can perform from the Book of Joshua. Act out the crossing of the Jordan River by following the instructions for crossing the Red Sea on page 19. But for this story, carry the ark across the water.

Ark of the Covenant

To learn more about the ark of the covenant, read Exodus 25:10-22.

1. Find a box about 15 inches long by 12 inches high by 12 inches deep.

2. Paint the outside of the box with gold spray paint or cover it with gold wrapping paper.

3. With wide tape, tape two long sticks (one stick on each side) to the long side of the box.

4. Place the tablet from the Moses story (page 17) inside the box.

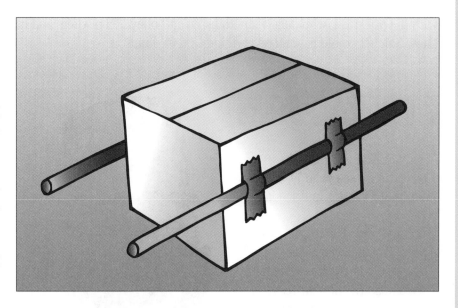

Walls of Jericho

- Build the walls of Jericho out of blocks or boxes and march around it like the Israelites.
- Make a trumpet by sticking a funnel in one end of an empty paper towel tube.
- Read the story of Rahab and the Israelite spies in Joshua 2:1-23 and 6:22-25. Ask a friend to play the part of Rahab who believed in God. Hang a red strip of cloth or string from your walls of Jericho as a sign for the Israelite spies.

Remember God takes care of those who trust in Him.

The Story of Achan

Read Joshua 6:24–7:26

- Act out this story by making a tent where Achan hid the treasures.
- Cover some coins, jewelry, and dishes with a towel.
- Wad up some paper to represent the rocks used to stone Achan. Remember it is always best to obey God in everything.

Which Bible character had no parents?

Joshua, son of Nun.

CAUTION

Have adult supervision when using spray paint.

Be strong and very courageous. Be careful to obey all the law my servant Moses gave you; do not turn from it to the right or to the left, that you may be successful wherever you go.

Joshua 1:7

Samuel and Eli

Casting Call This story needed a character who could listen carefully. Samuel lived with the priest Eli, who taught him to listen and obey. Then when God called Samuel, He knew Samuel would listen to everything God told him.

Wardrobe

Samuel: You will need the basic tunic (see page 7), a long scrap of material, and sandals.

Eli the Priest: Basic tunic (see page 7), gold rope, ice-cream tub, gold spray paint, white felt, white material or pillowcase, craft jewels, gold trim or braid and glue.

CAUTION

Have adult supervision when using spray paint.

Eli the Priest

The priests wore special clothing that represented the glory of God. To learn more about the garments that the priests wore, read Exodus 28:1-43.

1 Blue would be the best color for Eli's tunic, but any color will work. Tie it with a gold rope that you can get in a fabric store.

2 Make a priestly hat by spray painting an ice-cream tub gold. Glue craft jewels on the front. Or wrap it with a white piece of material or pillowcase to look like a white turban.

3 Make a breastplate. (See instructions below.)

4 The Word of God was written on scrolls. Make a scroll by rolling up a piece of paper first from the right side to the center, then from the left side to the center. Both rolls should curl toward the center and meet.

In the Old Testament, a priest was a man who was chosen to serve God in God's house. The priest offered sacrifices for the people so that God would forgive their sins. The New Testament tells us that we have a new high priest, Jesus. Jesus offered His life on the cross as a sacrifice for our sins.

The Breastplate

Each of the priest's garments represented something important. The precious gems on the breastplate stood for the twelve tribes of Israel, God's chosen people.

1 You will need two 12-inch square pieces of white felt and two 6 inch by 2 inch strips of white felt.

2 Cut three strips 12 inches long out of gold braid found in the fabric store.

3 On one piece of the felt, glue the gold braid horizontally three inches apart.

4 In between each row, glue three craft jewels, three inches apart.

5 Cut two strips of felt 6 inches by 2 inches. Glue the ends of each strip onto the felt squares so that they form a bib.

Collecting Details

What did the twelve jewels on the priest's breastplate represent?

(Exodus 39:14)

Samuel was a prophet and became the priest after Eli died. What other job did he have?

(1 Samuel 7:15)

Additional Props:

● Broom for Samuel to clean the tabernacle
● Bedroll or blanket.
● Bowls (See if Mom has gold or silver colored bowls.)

Samuel and Eli

Hannah loved God very much. Yet Hannah was very sad because she had no children. One day while visiting God's house she prayed, "Dear God, please give me a son. If You do, I will give him back to You to be Your helper."

The Priest Eli heard Hannah crying and said, "Don't cry. God will answer your prayer."

Hannah was so happy. She went back home believing God would answer her prayer. God soon gave Hannah a son. She named him Samuel. Hannah was so thankful that God answered her prayer.

Hannah remembered her promise to God. She taught Samuel all about God. She made sure that he would make a good helper for God. And when he was old enough, she took young Samuel to God's house to serve the priest and God.

Hannah told Eli the priest, "Remember the day you found me crying? Here is the son I prayed for. Now I have brought him back to be God's helper and to live with you in God's house."

Samuel loved being God's helper. He helped Eli keep God's house clean. He helped the old priest carry the scrolls that told of God's laws and promises. He watched as the people came and asked the priest to offer sacrifices for their sins. Samuel obeyed Eli and was a good helper.

One night after Samuel had gone to bed, he heard a voice call his name, "Samuel, Samuel."

Samuel jumped out of bed and ran to Eli. "Did you call me?"

"No, I didn't call you," said Eli. "Go back to bed, Samuel."

Again Samuel heard the voice call, "Samuel!" Again he ran to Eli's bedside.

"Eli, did you call me?" Samuel asked the priest. But Eli had not called the boy.

The voice called a third time, "Samuel, Samuel."

This time the old priest knew that God was calling Samuel's name. Eli told the young boy, "Go lie down on your bed. When you hear the voice, tell God that you are listening."

Samuel obeyed Eli and slipped back into his bed. Soon God called him. Samuel answered, "I am listening, God."

God told Samuel important things that would happen in the future. Samuel listened very carefully to everything God said. At an early age, Samuel chose to listen to God, and he grew to become a respected prophet of the Lord to God's people.

—Taken from 1 Samuel 1–3

Think ABOUT THIS

Why would God choose to speak to Samuel?

How can you be God's helper?

Setting the Scene

God gave Moses instructions for building a holy tent called a tabernacle. This special place of worship could be carried wherever the Israelites traveled. Later when they settled in the Promised Land, the tabernacle stayed in one place and the people came to worship God there.

The Tabernacle

1 Make a holy tent by taping or tacking up sheets in one corner of a room. If that's not possible, use a card table and drape a sheet over it for your holy tent.

2 Build an altar out of a box and place it outside the tent. Put a sacrifice lamb on the altar (see page 15).

3 Place the ark of the covenant inside the tent. (See page 23.)

4 Read Exodus 25-30 to find out more about the tabernacle

Samuel in the Temple

1 Act out Samuel helping Eli work hard in the holy tent.

2 Make a bed for Samuel out of blankets and pillows on one side of the stage. Have a friend act out Eli and make him a bed on the other side of the stage.

3 Whoever pretends to be Samuel can run to Eli's bed three times when he hears God's voice.

Samuel Becomes a Priest

As Samuel grew into a man, he became a priest like Eli. He helped the people and gave them wisdom from God. Later he helped God choose a king for Israel.

Read 1 and 2 Samuel to find out more about the wonderful things Samuel did for God and the people of Israel.

Jesus, Our High Priest

In the Old Testament, a priest was a man who was chosen to serve in God's house. The priest offered sacrifices for the people so that God would forgive their sins. The New Testament tells us that we have new high priest, Jesus. He offered His life on the cross as a sacrifice for our sins. Read the ninth chapter of Hebrews to find out more about Jesus, our high priest.

What is sometimes white, black, or brown, but should always be red?

The Bible.

I will listen to what God the LORD will say.

Psalm 85:8a

David and Goliath

Casting Call The Israelites had a big problem. A giant, named Goliath, was threatening to kill them all. It would take someone who put all his trust in God to fight this man. Young David was just right for the part. He had always trusted God and would trust Him now to fight the giant.

Wardrobe

Boy David: You will need a basic tunic (see page 7), sheep skin material, rope, cardboard, and rubber bands. Put on your basic tunic. Drape a piece of sheep skin material across your chest and pin it at shoulder and waist.

Goliath: Goliath was a giant, so you might want to pick the largest kid in your group for this part. You will need your tunic (see page 7), a thick belt, brown face makeup, an orange crate from a fruit box, felt scraps, string, silver spray paint, broomstick, cardboard, aluminum serving tray, aluminum foil, cardboard, strong tape, and boots.

CAUTION

Have adult supervision when using spray paint.

David's Sling

You can use felt or any type of material to make a sling, but vinyl works nicely.

1 Draw a pattern of a sling on a piece of paper. It will have a 3-inch square patch in the middle and two strips on either side of the patch.

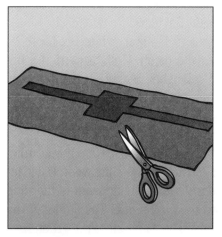

2 Use this pattern to cut out a sling on the material you choose.

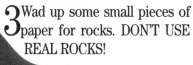

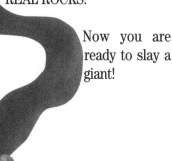

3 Wad up some small pieces of paper for rocks. DON'T USE REAL ROCKS!

Now you are ready to slay a giant!

Goliath

1 Make a tunic (see page 7). Pull it up or pin up the bottom so that it is shorter. Warriors wore shorter clothing. Wearing a thick belt or rope around your waist will help pull up the tunic.

2 Make a spear by taking the bristles off an old broomstick. Paint the broomstick with silver spray paint. Cut a spear head out of cardboard and cover it with foil. Tape it to one end of the broomstick.

3 Make a shield out of an aluminum serving tray. You can buy these at the grocery store. Tape a 2-inch by 6-inch strip of cardboard on one side of the tray for a handle. You can also use a large aluminum pan lid. Or cut a large circle out of poster board and cover it with aluminum foil.

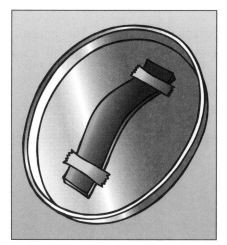

4 Make some armor out of fruit crates following the instructions below.

5 If you have an old sports helmet, spray paint it silver to make a helmet.

6 Give yourself a beard by coloring your chin with brown or black face makeup. Or borrow your mom's eyebrow pencil. Dampen the tip of the pencil and color your chin so you look mean and scruffy.

7 Make a sword like the one on page 21.

8 Put on your biggest boots. Or borrow some boots from a grown-up, so your feet look really big.

Now you're ready to lead the Philistines into battle!

Armor

You can find fruit trays free at the grocery store or fruit market.

1 Paint two fruit trays with silver spray paint.

2 Cut out two straps out of felt to go over your shoulders. Glue the straps to the inside of the top ends of the trays.

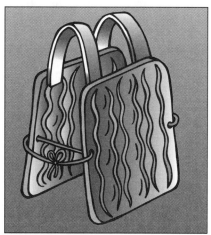

3 Punch small holes halfway down the sides of the fruit trays. Tie a string at each hole. This will tie the armor around your waist.

David Slays Goliath

David was a young Hebrew boy who loved God. His father owned a lot of sheep, and David would watch over them in the fields. At night David would play his harp and sing to comfort his sheep.

Many times David had to save the sheep from wild animals. He carried a sling so that he was ready at all times to protect his sheep. It was a simple weapon made from a small leather patch with two long straps. David would place a small rock in the patch and swing the sling over his head. Letting go of one of the straps sent the rock flying. David killed a lion and a bear with his sling.

One day David's father called him from the fields. "I want you to take some food to your brothers. They are at battle with the Philistines."

David quickly ran to the battlefield. But he was surprised to find his brothers were not fighting. The entire Israelite army was hiding and afraid!

"What's going on?" David asked.

"The Philistines had a secret weapon!" his brothers said.

"A secret weapon? What is it?" David asked.

"Watch and see," they answered.

So David waited to see the "secret weapon" that his brothers feared so much. Soon the ground began to shake. An enemy soldier walked out to the front lines. Not just any man, but a giant named Goliath!

"Send your best man out to fight me," he roared.

No one moved a muscle. They were all too scared, except young David. David told the Israelite army, "Why are you afraid? I will fight the giant. God is on our side!"

The king heard that David was not afraid of Goliath, so he sent for the boy. "You're just a boy. What makes you think you can fight this giant?"

"God helped me kill a lion and a bear. God will help me kill this giant!" said David.

David marched out to Goliath, while his brothers and the army hid in the camp. Goliath carried a big sword and spear. He laughed when he saw the boy, "Ha! You are just a pup! I will feed you to the birds!"

David yelled, "You come to me with a sword and spear. I come to you in the name of the Lord."

David picked up five small stones. He put one stone in his sling. Around and around his sling went. David let go of the sling. *Whoosh!* The stone flew out of the sling and went flying into the air. *Smack!* The stone hit the giant's forehead! *Thud!* The giant fell to the ground!

David ran over to Goliath. He picked up the giant's heavy sword and cut off his head. "God gave me victory!" David cried.

The Israelites cheered and shouted. They chased the enemy army. David trusted in God to help him face his battles! We can trust God too.

—Taken from 1 Samuel 17

Think ABOUT THIS

Do you have a giant problem in your life?

What can you learn from this story about how to solve it?

Setting the Scene

Start the story with David in the fields watching over his sheep. Then move the scene to the battlefield with Goliath.

David's Harp

1 Draw a harp on a piece of cardboard or heavy poster board. Make it about 12 inches long and 15 inches wide in the middle. YOU MAY NEED AN ADULT TO HELP YOU WITH THE CUTTING.

2 Ask an adult to help you punch six holes along the straight side of the harp. Now punch holes directly across on the other side of the harp.

3 Cut six long rubber bands in half. Use big thick rubber bands that will stretch really well. Tie the ends of one rubber band to connect each set of holes.

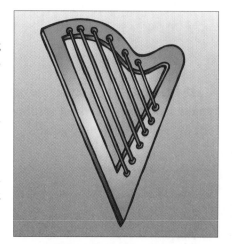

The Shepherd's Field

1 Scatter some plants around to make it look like the outdoors. Or you can make a moon and some stars and hang them from the ceiling to pretend you are David watching the sheep at night.

2 Have a friend dress up in a lion costume like the one on page 37. The lion can pretend to be trying to steal the sheep, while David chases it away with his sling. Remember David killed the lion, so the lion has to fall down dead!

The Battlefield

1 Move the plants around so it looks like a different area.

2 In one corner of the stage drape a sheet over a card table to represent the king's tent.

3 Lay a blue sheet or blanket on the floor for a small stream where David will pick up his stones.

Hint: If you decide to video record your David and Goliath skit, have your camera man shoot Goliath from an angle on the floor. That will make Goliath really look like a giant!

Where did Goliath receive some bad news?

Right between the eyes.

Sheep

David was a shepherd so you will need at least one sheep. You can make a pillow sheep like the one on page 15. Or make a sheep costume using the animal pattern on page 37. Use a white tunic and some white socks. Apply black face paint on your nose to achieve a cute lamb costume.

How tall was Goliath?
(1 Samuel 17:4)

How many brothers did David have?
(1 Samuel 17:12–14)

FROM THE
Script

I call to the LORD, who is worthy of praise, and I am saved from my enemies.
Psalm 18:3

King Solomon and Two Women

Casting Call Playing the part of a king takes someone with a lot of wisdom. Solomon tried out for the part and got it. He didn't care about riches or power, just wisdom to guide God's people.

Wardrobe

King Solomon: You will need your basic tunic (see page 7). Kings wore royal colors of purple and red. If your basic tunic is a different color, you can drape purple cloth across your body or you can make another coat tunic. (See page 12.) You will need jewelry, poster board, gold foil paper, craft jewels, and glue.

Two Women: You will need two basic tunics (see page 7) or robes, shawls, and a doll.

A King's Crown

You will need poster board, gold foil paper, and craft jewels.

1 Glue a sheet of foil paper onto a piece of poster board.

2 Measure around your head to find the size you will need for your crown.

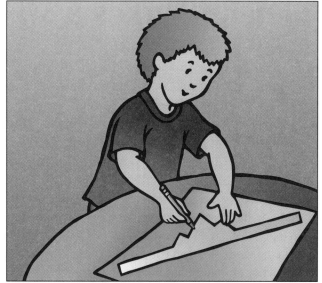

3 Draw a three-point design on the back of the poster board.

4 Cut out crown and glue craft jewels on the front.

Two women

1 These two women were probably very poor, so don't add a lot of fancy things to their costumes.

2 Cover your heads with shawls or wrap a shawl around your shoulders.

3 They will fight over a baby in the story, so borrow a doll from your little sister or ask her to play one of the women.

Collecting Details

What biblical king wrote the book of Proverbs?

(*Proverbs 1:1*)

Where did the Lord appear to Solomon?

(*1 Kings 3:5*)

Additional Props

● Bedrolls for the women to sleep on.
● A sword like the one on page 21.
● Baby blanket to wrap doll in.

Solomon Makes a Wise Ruling

Solomon was King of Israel. He wanted to be a good king, so he asked God to help him rule well. One night God talked to Solomon in a dream. He said, "Ask me for anything you want and I will give it to you."

Solomon didn't have to think twice. "I don't care about riches. I don't care about having lots of land and great honors. I just want to rule the people well. Please give me wisdom to be a good king."

God was pleased that Solomon had asked for wisdom and not riches. He told Solomon, "You could have asked for all the money in the world. Instead you asked for wisdom, which is much better than riches. So I will also make you rich and you will have great honor among the people." Solomon did rule wisely and was a good king.

One day two women came to the king's court. They had an argument that they wanted Solomon to settle.

One woman cried, "Dear King, I live in the same house as this woman. I had a baby boy while she lived with me. When my child was three days old, she had a son too. We were all alone in the house. During the night this woman's little boy died. When she found her son dead, she got up in the night and took my son from my side. She put her dead child where my baby lay."

"That's a lie! Her baby died!" the other woman held a baby in her arms and shouted as she pointed her finger at the first woman.

"Silence! Let her finish her story," King Solomon ordered.

The first woman continued, "When I woke up, I found my son dead! But then I looked closer and realized it wasn't my baby at all! It was hers! She had my son!"

"No, the dead one is yours. This child is mine," she insisted as she held the baby tighter.

The two women cried and argued before the king. Solomon listened as they shouted back and forth. God had promised to give Solomon wisdom, so the king came up with a good idea to find out which woman was the true mother.

"How can I know which one of you tells the truth? Bring me a sword," the king told his guard.

The guard brought Solomon a big sword. "Cut the baby in two! Give each woman one half of the child! That should end this argument!"

The first mother cried, "No! Please don't kill my son! Give him to her! I would rather he be alive with her than dead!"

The other woman sneered, "Good idea, then neither of us will have him. Cut him in two!"

King Solomon knew just what to do. "Give the living baby to the first woman. Do not kill him. She cares for him more than the other woman. She must be the true mother!"

When all of the people heard this story, they knew that God had given Solomon great wisdom! God gives wisdom to anyone who asks for it.

—*Taken from 1 Kings 3:16–28*

Think ABOUT THIS

Would you like to have the wisdom that Solomon had?

How can you get wisdom too?

Setting the Scene

King Solomon lived in the palace. He made his wise rulings from his throne, but he also traveled among his people in a carriage. There are several scenes that you can use in this story.

Solomon's Throne Room

1. Build a throne room for King Solomon. Throw a blanket or sheet over a chair.

2. Lay out some towels before the chair like a rug.

3. Place some plants on either side of the chair.

Solomon's Carriage

1. Read Song of Songs 3:9-10 to find out what Solomon's carriage looked like.

2. Instead of covering a chair with sheets, cover it with pillows with purple covers.

3. Pretend that the women come to Solomon's carriage instead of the throne room.

Solomon's Scepter

1. Wrap an empty paper towel tube with aluminum foil. Use a wrapping paper tube for a longer scepter.

2. Wad a large piece of foil into a ball. Glue it to the top of the paper towel tube. Or wrap foil around a Styrofoam ball.

3. Decorate the ball with jewels and glue it on the end of the tube.

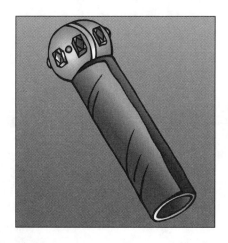

Solomon's Bedroom

The Lord appeared to Solomon in a dream.

1. Make a bedroll for Solomon.

2. On two pieces of poster board draw pictures that show the things God offered Solomon. One picture can be of lots of wealth and money. The other can be people bowing down to the kings.

3. Place the pictures behind Solomon to make it look like a dream.

FROM THE Script

If any of you lacks wisdom, he should ask God, who gives generously to all without finding fault, and it will be given to him.

James 1:5

Try this tongue twister:

Solomon sings sweet sounding songs at sunset.

Daniel in the Lions' Den

Casting Call The cast of this story included some evil men who did not believe in God. But the main character, Daniel, was faithful to always love and worship God, even to the point of being thrown into the den of hungry lions.

Wardrobe

Daniel: Your basic tunic (see page 7), cloak, and a beard if you want (see page 9).

Lion: Basic tunic, preferably brown, (see page 7), bath sized towels, matching wash cloths, masking tape, scissors, marker, safety pins, ribbons, old brown sock, and face makeup.

Animal Costume

1 Spread a regular bath sized towel out on a table. Fold one long edge of the towel upward about five inches. Tape the fold down with masking tape to keep it in place. Or Mom can sew it in place.

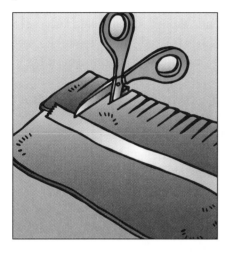

2 Cut three-inch slits one inch apart on the fold. Cut the fold ends apart to loosen the slits to make a floppy lion mane. Skip this step if you want to be a girl lion.

3 Drape the towel over your head. Keep the folded edge to the front. Look in a mirror and decide where you want the ears to be and mark those spots. Remove the towel and cut slits where you made each mark.

4 Fold the washcloth in half and cut up the fold.

5 Fold one washcloth piece in half. The top is the folded edge. Fold down the corners at the top, so that the corners meet in the center of the washcloth to make a pointy ear shape. Repeat this step with the other washcloth half.

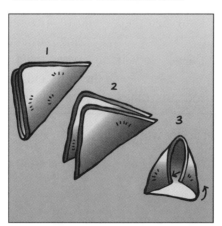

6 Push the bottom, flat edge of the ear through the slit in the towel so that the point of the ear is pointing up. Pin the flat edge of the ear to the inside of the towel with a safety pin. Repeat this step for the other ear.

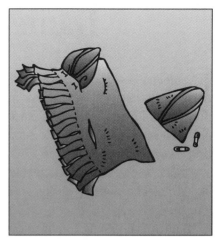

7 Put the towel back on your head and tie it in place with the string or ribbon.

8 Put your tunic on, covering up the extra towel around your shoulders or you can leave the towel out.

9 Make a long tail by stuffing your Dad's old brown sock with tissue paper. Ask someone to pin it to the backside of your tunic, at your tailbone.

10 Paint whiskers on your face and practice your roar.

Collecting Details

Who had a vision of a lion with eagles' wings?

(Daniel 7:1–4)

According to 1 Peter, who is like a hungry lion?

(1 Peter 5:8)

Daniel Always Obeyed God

Daniel had been taken captive in a foreign land. The people there did not believe in the one true God. But Daniel loved God and because he did, he always did what was right. He would bow down and pray to God three times every day.

Daniel worked in the king's courts. King Darius liked Daniel because he worked so hard and did a good job.

"Daniel, I am going to put you in charge of all my officials," said the king.

Soon the other officials became jealous of Daniel. "We cannot find anything wrong with this man. He works hard. He never lies or cheats or steals. He prays three times a day to his God. He makes the rest of us look bad," they all grumbled.

One of the men said, "The only way Daniel will disobey the king is if the law is against his God."

So they all went to the king and tricked him into making a new law. "Oh great King Darius. May you live forever! You should make a law that says that if anyone prays to any god or man during the next thirty days, they must be thrown in the den of lions."

Now the king was a prideful man, so he said, "Sounds good to me. I will sign this law of yours. Everyone will pray to me or into the lions' den they go!"

The men snickered, "Now we have Daniel. He will never stop praying to that God of his."

Daniel continued to pray to the true God three times a day. "I must obey God's law," he said.

Daniel's enemies listened and watched. "He will not pray to the king—you just wait and see."

When they heard Daniel praying to God and not the king, they rushed to King Darius. "Oh lord, there is one man who disobeys your law!"

"Who dares to disobey me?" shouted the king. "He will be the lions' dinner tonight!"

"It is Daniel," the men gloated.

"No! Not my friend Daniel!" cried King Darius. He realized that he had been tricked, but there was no way to change the law. Daniel must go into the dark lions' den.

"Daniel, I am sorry. I hope your God saves you from the mouths of the lions."

"Oh my king. My God will save me," Daniel said as the men threw him into the den and closed the door.

All night King Darius paced the floor. He could not sleep. "I hope Daniel is all right."

At the first light of dawn, King Darius ran to the lions' den. "Open the door!" he ordered. "Daniel, my friend, did your God save you?"

"King Darius, yes my God saved me," called Daniel. "He shut the mouths of these hungry lions. They are like little kittens."

"Get Daniel out of there!" shouted the king. "Now we will deal with these jealous men. Into the den they will go!" This time God opened the mouths of the lions.

King Darius was overjoyed and said, "From now on everyone must fear and obey Daniel's God, for He is the true and living God!" Daniel's obedience helped others to believe in God too.

—*Taken from Daniel 6*

Think ABOUT THIS

God helped Daniel to do well, even though he was captive in a foreign land. Read Daniel chapters 1-6 to find out some more neat things God did for Daniel.

How do you think God will help you?

Setting the Scene

If you want to put on a full play of this story, divide the room or stage into three sections—the king's throne room, Daniel's room, and the lions' den. One kid can play King Darius and a couple of others can play the jealous officials.

King Darius' Room

The throne room can look like the one on page 35. King Darius should walk back and forth in his room, wringing his hands worrying about Daniel.

Daniel's Room

Daniel's room can be in one corner of the room or stage with a simple bed roll where Daniel will pray three times a day. Later in the story, while Daniel is in the lion's den, have the jealous officials laughing and drinking in this area. They are celebrating that they got rid of Daniel

The Lions' Den

1 Set some chairs up in a semicircle, with the seats turned away from the front.

2 Drape some dark blankets or sheets over the chairs leaving the front open.

3 Under the blankets, the lion waits for his dinner. If your chairs are too short to provide space, wedge a couple of broomsticks between them to hold the blanket up higher.

4 Make more than one lion costume, one with a mane and one without.

Set the stage so you have several things going on at once. Divide the stage or room into three sections with sheets. Daniel can sit in the lions' den praying to God. The lion can rub up against him like a kitten. King Darius can pace in the throne room all night. And the men can sit in Daniel's room laughing and celebrating.

Q: Why were the lions in the den the center of attention?

A: Because they were the mane attraction.

We must obey God rather than men!

Acts 5:29b

Queen Esther and Mordecai

Casting Call God's people were in trouble. It would take a brave person to stand before the king to save them. Esther accepted the part and bravely asked the king to spare the Israelites. Her courage and faith in God saved her people.

Wardrobe

Queen Esther: You will need a basic tunic (see page 7). You can make a "royal" tunic out of purple material and use it for queens and kings. Or make the "queenly" dress shown on page 41. You can make a crown like on page 33 or on page 60. Wear a few jewels and put your hair in a pretty braid or bun.

Mordecai: The basic tunic (see page 7), rags, safety pins, and baby powder.

1 Ask Mom for a pretty colored sheet. It should be a solid color, since they didn't have prints in Bible times. You will also need about 12 feet of cord.

2 Measure from your neck to your feet. This is the length of the front of this costume. Take that measurement and mark from one end of the sheet to the center. Make a small mark at this point.

3 Cut a slit at this mark big enough for your head to go through.

4 Slip the sheet over your head and stick your arms straight out. Have a friend fit the sheet to fall evenly around your body, with longer material in the back.

5 Put the middle of the cord around your neck. Wrap the cord over your shoulders and under your arms. Cross the cord in the back and wrap around your waist.

6 Cross the front of your waist and then back again and then tie it in the front.

Mordecai

Mordecai becomes very sad in this story. To show how upset he was, Mordecai dressed in torn clothes and ashes.

1 Pin some old torn rags to your tunic before slipping it on to make your tunic look ragged. Or drape a ragged shawl around your shoulders.

2 Shake baby powder in your hair to look like you poured ashes on your head.

Additional Props

● A scepter like the one on page 35 for King Xerxes, Esther's husband.
● A hand mirror, brush, and comb for Esther.
● Bowls of fruit, dishes, and cups for Esther's special dinner.

Collecting Details

What did Esther ask Mordecai and all the Jews in Susa to do for her?

(Esther 4:15–16)

Who was supposed to hang on the gallows that Haman died on?

(Esther 7:9–10)

Esther Saves Her People

King Xerxes wanted a wife. So he looked for the most beautiful girls in the land. They came to the palace so he could choose a new wife. Esther was a beautiful girl who lived with her cousin, Mordecai. He knew that Esther would be chosen queen. Mordecai loved her like a daughter and feared for her life.

He warned her, "Do not tell anyone that you are a Hebrew. There are many people who do not like our people. They do not want us to worship the true God."

Esther left her home and went to the palace with the other girls. As soon as King Xerxes saw Esther, he fell in love with her. She remembered what Mordecai told her and never told anyone her nationality.

In the king's court there was a man who hated the Hebrew people. Haman wanted to kill all the Israelites in the land. He tricked the king into making a law to do just that. He especially hated Mordecai because he refused to bow down at his feet.

Mordecai became really upset. He wore torn clothes and put ashes on his head to show how sad he felt. When Esther heard that Mordecai was sad, she sent a servant to ask what was wrong.

"Tell Esther that Haman plans to kill every last one of the Hebrews. Even you will be killed. God has put you in the king's palace to save your people," Mordecai said to the servant. "Tell her she must stop Haman."

When Esther received the message, she became very frightened. *How can I help my people? I cannot go before the king unless he calls me. If he is unhappy with me, the king can have me put to death,* Esther thought.

Beautiful Esther prayed for three days, asking God for courage. Then she put on her prettiest dress, held her breath, and knocked on the door of the king's court.

When King Xerxes saw Esther he thought, *Why is my wife here? She knows that coming without permission can bring her death. But she does look very beautiful.* So he raised his scepter and gave her permission to speak.

Trembling, Esther asked, "My lord, I would like to invite you to a special dinner. Please bring Haman, too."

The king answered, "We would be happy to join you, Esther. Thank you."

King Xerxes and Haman went to Esther's dinner and had a good time. So Esther invited them again. But this time Esther asked the king, "Please grant me one request."

"Esther, you can have anything you want up to half my kingdom," replied King Xerxes.

"Please spare my life and the lives of my people," Esther said. " Haman is plotting to kill all the Hebrews, and I am one too."

King Xerxes became very angry and ordered Haman hanged. He then made a new law that saved God's people. The king made Mordecai an official in his court, because he realized that he was good man. King Xerxes loved Esther very much. God put her in a special place and time so that she could help her people. God has a special plan for everyone.

—*Taken from the Book of Esther*

Think ABOUT THIS

How did Esther face her problem?

What can you do when you have a big problem?

Setting the Scene

Start your story in the home of Mordecai, then move to the palace where Esther became queen.

Mordecai's Home

1 This would have been a very humble dwelling with just a few pieces of furniture. A small table and a couple of chairs will do. Place a few dishes on the table.

2 Esther can wear a tunic and a shawl. Mordecai can wear a tunic without the rags for this scene.

Esther's Palace Room

Read Esther 2:12-15 to find out how Esther spent a whole year making herself beautiful for the king.

1 Put on the "queenly" costume.

2 Set the scene of Esther's room by draping sheets over furniture and placing large plants and pots around.

3 Esther can pretend to make herself beautiful by looking in the mirror and brushing her hair.

4 Later in the story, Esther will weep and pray for her people from this room.

King Xerxes' Throne Room

1 Have a friend dress up as King Xerxes using a costume similar to the one of King Solomon, page 32. Make sure that King Xerxes has a beautiful scepter for the story (see page 35).

2 Another friend can play Haman by dressing up in a simple tunic and robe.

3 Set the scene for Esther's special dinners by spreading out a tablecloth or sheet on the floor. Set glasses and plates around the cloth. Put a bowl of fruit in the center.

4 Spread out large pillows around the tablecloth. Set plants around the room so that it looks like a special palace room.

How many books in the Old Testament were named after Esther?

Twenty-two- the rest were named before Esther.

So we say with confidence, "The Lord is my helper; I will not be afraid. What can man do to me?"

Hebrews 13:6

The Birth of Jesus

Casting Call God needed a special person who would be willing to obey Him. An angel asked Mary if she wanted the part. She joyfully accepted and obeyed. She soon became the mother of God's Son, Jesus.

Wardrobe

Mary: A basic tunic (see page 7) and a shawl.

Joseph: A basic tunic (see page 7), a bathrobe ,and an eyebrow pencil or face paint.

Angel: A basic tunic (see page 7) preferably white. Or wrap a white sheet around your tunic, poster board, white craft feathers, gold trim, glitter, glue, gold rope or chain, safety pins, gold garland or gold ribbon.

Collecting Details

Jesus had another name that meant, "God is with us?" What was it?

(Matthew 1:23)

What was the name of the angel who visited Mary?

(Luke 1:26)

Mary

Wear the basic tunic and cover your head with a shawl.

Joseph

1. Wear basic tunic.

2. Borrow Dad's bathrobe or wear a cloak over your tunic.

3. Joseph was young, so color a beard on your chin with an eyebrow pencil or face paint.

Angel

1. You will need two sheets of white poster board.

2. Draw one wing on each piece of the posterboard.

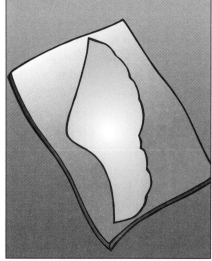

3. Cut out the wings.

4. You can glue white craft feathers, gold trim, glitter or anything else that seems angelic onto your wings. Or you can just leave them white.

5. Put on your tunic (or sheet) and tie it with gold chains or ropes. Have a friend pin the wings on your back with several safety pins.

6. Make a halo out of a gold garland found at a craft store or tie gold ribbon around your head.

Go out and spread the good news about the Christ child!

Mother: How was Sunday School?

Bobby: It was good. We learned about the birth of Jesus. But I just have one question.

Mother: What is it?

Bobby: Why did Jesus always do things on holidays like Christmas and Easter?

Additional Props

● A small baby doll.
● A pot that Mary could be carrying when the angel comes to her.
● A bedroll for Joseph to be sleeping on when he has his dream.

The Angel Brings Good News

Mary lived in Nazareth. She was a young woman, engaged to a carpenter named Joseph. They were ordinary people, but God chose them for His special plan.

One day an angel came to Mary to tell her a message from God. The angel frightened Mary at first.

"Do not be afraid. God has chosen you to become the mother of a special child. This boy will be named Jesus. He will be the Son of God," the angel said.

"How can this be? I am not married yet." asked Mary.

"By God's power and Holy Spirit you will have a child," said the angel. "God will be the Father of your Son."

Mary was happy at this news. For a long time, her people had talked about a Savior who would come to help them. Now she would be the mother of God's Son. "I am the Lord's servant," she said. "I will do whatever God wants me to do."

Then the angel left Mary. She was so happy that she danced around the room and sang a song. She thanked God for choosing her to become the mother of the special baby boy.

Mary told Joseph what the angel said. Joseph became worried about taking Mary as his wife. He wasn't sure he believed her story. And he didn't like the idea of her having a baby before they were married. So he decided to break off their engagement.

But God wanted Joseph to raise Jesus as his own son and prepare Him for the work that God planned for the boy. Joseph came from the family of David and God wanted Jesus to be part of that family. So God sent the angel to help Joseph to believe Mary's story.

While he was sleeping, the angel appeared to him in a dream.

"Joseph, son of David, do not be afraid. What Mary told you is true. Take her as your wife because God's Son will need someone to help take care of Him. Name the boy Jesus, which means Savior, because He will save His people from their sins."

Joseph was happy that the angel had brought such good news. He went to Mary and took her as his wife.

The king of the land made a law that everyone should travel to their hometown to be counted. So Mary and Joseph went to a town called Bethlehem. It was a hard trip because Mary's baby was soon to be born. When they arrived in Bethlehem, they found the city crowded with people. They went from door to door, inn to inn, looking for a place to stay.

"Sorry, we are all full!" every innkeeper told them. Finally one innkeeper noticed that Mary was going to have her baby soon. "I have no rooms left, but you can use my stable. You must get your wife out of the cold," the innkeeper told Joseph.

Mary and Joseph quickly settled down in the stable. Soon the baby was born. Mary wrapped the child in swaddling clothes and handed Him to Joseph. Joseph named the boy Jesus just as the angel had said.

They made a bed for Jesus in the manger where the animals ate their straw. Mary and Joseph were happy as they watched the Son of God sleep quietly. The angel watched over them, rejoicing that God had brought the Savior into the world.

—Taken from Matthew 1:18–25,
Luke 1:26-56; 2:1–7

Jesus' birth was special to the entire world. List some reasons why you think His birth was so special.

Jesus' name was special because it told the reason He was born. Your name is special too. Ask your parents why they chose your name for you.

Setting the Scene

This story has many different settings to tell the story besides the stable where Jesus was born. Start your story in Mary's home, then with Joseph's dream.

Mary's House

Set the stage for the appearance of the angel to Mary.

1 Put a small table and chair in the middle of the stage. Have Mary working in her home.

2 Shine a bright light on one corner of the stage and have the angel come out of the light.

Joseph's House

1 Have Joseph lay down on a bed roll on the floor.

2 Draw a picture of a baby on a poster board. Hang the poster above Joseph's head. Shine a bright light on the poster as someone off stage tells Joseph the news about Mary's special baby.

The Ride to Bethlehem

1 Place two tall stools close together.

2 Cover the stools with a gray or brown sheet.

3 Draw the head of a donkey on a piece of cardboard. Cut the head out and tape it to one end of the covered stools.

4 Have Mary sit side saddle on the covered bar stools to look like she is riding a donkey to Bethlehem.

The Stable

In Bible times caves were used for stables for animals. Have you ever been in a cave? They are cold and dark. The manger was where the owner of the animals would put the hay or feed for the animals.

1 Set the scene by setting up two ladders the same height and about six feet apart from each other.

2 Drape dark light weight blankets or sheets over the ladders connecting them. Leave the front open so it looks like a cave.

3 A large basket or box can work as the manger. Cut up strips of yellow and brown construction paper to look like straw.

4 Wrap a doll in strips of cloth to look like the baby Jesus.

More Ideas

● If you want to put on a complete play of the story of the Birth of Jesus ask some friends to join you. Ask one kid to dress up like a sheep using the instructions on page 37. You could make a cow costume using tan towels and a string for a tail.

● Spread the strips of yellow and brown construction paper all over the stage or go to a local garden store for some real straw.

● Shine a light behind the manger to show that the baby was special.

FROM THE
Script

For God so loved the world that he gave his one and only Son, that whoever believes in him shall not perish but have eternal life.

John 3:16

The Shepherds and Wise Men Visit Bethlehem

Casting Call God wanted to tell the world that His Son was born. So He chose some special people who He knew would be glad to hear the good news. The shepherds and wise men were so excited to see the baby Jesus that they went out rejoicing and telling others the good news.

Wardrobe

Shepherds: If you put on a full play, you will want at least two shepherds for this part. Put on the basic tunic (see page 7), fur scraps or a cloak and a head drape like on page 7.

Magi or Wise Men: The basic tunic (see page 7), purple cloth, gold ropes, crowns (see page 33 or page 60), or head covering like on page 7, and jewelry.

Try saying this tongue twister fast three times:

Shepherds seldom shear sheep in shady sheds.

Shepherds

1 Put on the basic tunic. Wrap a piece of fur across your front or drape a cloak over your shoulders. Or a robe works great too.

2 Wear a head drape.

3 Carry a broomstick or long tree limb for a staff.

4 Your shepherds can wear beards or go without. (See page 9 or page 7).

5 The Shepherds were excited at the good news they heard.

Magi or Wise Men

These men may have been kings from a far away land or men who studied the stars. Because they brought three gifts, scholars usually say there were three wise men. All we really know is that there was more than one. And whoever they were, these men were wealthy. They brought the baby Jesus expensive gifts.

1 Dress in your basic tunic. Add purple cloth or gold ropes to your tunic.

2 Wear a crown that you make or buy at the craft store. Or wear a head covering tied with gold rope or trim.

3 You can wear a beard (see page 9 or page 17).

4 Like the Shepherds, they will need to act happy to see the baby Jesus.

The shepherds went to town of David. What was its name?
(Luke 2:15)

From which direction did the wise men see the star?
(Matthew 2:2)

Additional Props

- Sheep like on page 15.
- Gifts for the Christ child from the Magi can be a small pretty box or vase.
- Cut circles from yellow paper or use some play money for the gold they brought Jesus.

The Good News Spreads

While Mary and Joseph were still in the stable, the angel of the Lord appeared to shepherds in the hills near Bethlehem. At first the shepherds were afraid.

"What is that bright light in the sky?" the shepherds shouted.

"Do not be afraid," said the angel. "I have good news! Tonight in the town of Bethlehem a child was born."

"A child?" asked the shepherds. They wondered why the birth of a child should be good news.

"The Savior, Christ the Lord, has been born. Go and you will find him wrapped in cloth, lying in a manger," the angel answered.

Suddenly the sky filled with angels. They were all singing songs of praise for sending Jesus the Savior. "Glory to God in the highest, and on earth peace to men on whom his favor rests," they sang.

Just as quickly as the angel appeared, the sky grew dark once again. "We must hurry to Bethlehem to find this Christ child," the shepherds all agreed.

When they found the child in the stable, they knew that He was indeed the Savior. They left rejoicing and told others the good news.

God wanted the whole world to know that Jesus had been born. So He put a bright star in the sky announcing His birth. Some wise men that studied the stars saw this bright star in the sky. "We must follow this star," they said. "It will lead us to a special king."

So the wise men made the long trip across the desert. When they came to the town of Jerusalem, they went straight to King Herod. "Do you know where the new king has been born?" they asked.

King Herod knew of no other king, but he knew that prophets of old had said that a king would be born in Bethlehem. Herod was angry at the thought of a new king, so he pretended not to know where the baby might be found. "Go and when you find this new king, come and tell me where He is, so that I can worship Him too."

The wise men left King Herod and this time the star led them to the town of Bethlehem, right to the baby Jesus. When they saw the child, they bowed down and worshiped Him.

"This truly is a special child who will save the world," they said, overjoyed. They gave Jesus expensive gifts of gold, incense, and myrrh. They wanted to show Him that they loved and worshiped Him.

Before the wise men returned across the desert, God warned them in a dream. "Do not go back to King Herod. He wants to hurt Jesus." So they went home another way.

They left rejoicing. Like the shepherds, they wanted to tell the good news to everyone they met. "A Savior has been born!"

—*Taken from Luke 2:8–20; Matthew 2:1–12*

The wise men were really called Magi. How can we truly be "wise men?"

Why is the birth of Jesus important for your life?

Setting the Scene

This story has several scenes, including the shepherd fields and the stable. You can tell this story as part of The Birth of Jesus that begins on page 44. Read the first few chapters of the books of Matthew, Mark, and Luke to find out details that you could use to put on a play.

Shepherds' Field

1 Set the scene for the shepherds in the fields by spreading out some blankets and plants around the room or stage.

2 Make some pillow sheep (see page 15) or have one person dress up like a sheep (see page 37).

3 Darken the room. Suddenly have the angel appear as you turn a bright light on him or her. Since you may not have a lot of people in your play, you can add more lights to represent the other angels.

4 Have your angel stand on a sturdy chair so he or she is above the shepherds.

Camels

Since the Magi or wise men traveled a great distance to see the Christ child, they probably traveled on camels across the desert.

1 Draw some camel heads on some poster board.

2 Tape the heads onto broomsticks.

3 Have the wise men ride across the desert on their camels.

Moving Star

1 Cut a large star out of poster board or cardboard and cover it with aluminum foil.

2 Securely tape a large paper clip to the back and top of the star to make a hook.

3 Stretch a long piece of fishing thread or other strong thin thread across the room, with thread going through the paper clip of the star.

4 Attach another piece of thread to one side of the star.

5 Gently pull the star with the attached thread across the room. Have the wise men follow the star.

King Herod

Have one person participating in your play dress like King Herod. Remember he will pretend to like the news about Jesus, but is really angry inside. After the wise men find Jesus, have them bed down for the night. Ask someone from behind the stage speak to them about not going back to King Herod.

. . . .

More ideas

● Set up a stable like on page 47 on one corner of the stage.
● Have the wise men traveling in the far corner of the other side of the stage.
● The Shepherd's field can be located in the center.

FROM THE
Script

Today in the town of David a Savior has been born to you; he is Christ the Lord.

Luke 2:11

Jesus Begins His Ministry

Casting Call When Jesus began His ministry, He needed people who would be committed to following Him. Because of his faith in God, John the Baptist fit the role of preparing the way for Jesus. Fishermen who were willing to obey and commit their lives to Christ left their nets and followed Him.

Wardrobe

Jesus: Basic tunic preferably white (see page 7), long piece of blue material or sheet, a cloth belt, and eyebrow pencil or face paint.

John the Baptist: Basic tunic (see page 7) preferably a black or brown one, fur material, and eyebrow pencil or face paint.

Fishermen: Basic tunic (see page 7), fish netting, cardboard, and scissors.

Jesus

Most illustrations show Jesus wearing a white tunic with a blue cloak. Tie a piece of cloth around your waist like a belt. Drape a blue cloak or piece of material across your chest. Use the eyebrow pencil to color a beard on your face.

John the Baptist

Here's what the Bible says about John's clothing in Matthew 3:4 "John's clothes were made of camel's hair, and he had a leather belt around his waist. His food was locusts and wild honey."

1 Make a camel hair cloak out of fake fur that you can buy at a fabric store. This material is not usually as wide as the tunic material so you will only get one tunic out of it.

2 The camel hair cloak will come down about half way between your waist and knees. Measure from the top of your shoulder to that point. Double that

number and that will be the length of the material.

3 To make the cloak, follow the basic tunic instructions. After closing up the sides of the tunic either with tape or by sewing, cut out one of the arms.

4 Tie a piece of leather rope around your waist or put on a thick leather belt.

5 Draw a beard on your face with the eyebrow pencil or face paint.

Fisherman

Several of Jesus' disciples were fishermen along the Sea of Galilee.

1 Dress in the basic tunic.

2 You can find fish netting at a craft store or sporting goods store.

3 Draw and cut out some fish from cardboard. Scatter the fish throughout the net.

4 Drape the net across your shoulders.

Additional Props
- Rubber grasshoppers.
- Honey comb.
- A basket for holding fish.

Collecting Details

In what river was Jesus baptized by John?
(Matthew 3:13)

Who was in the boat with James and John when Jesus called them to follow Him?
(Matthew 4:21)

Jesus Has Many Friends

The time came for Jesus to begin His ministry. He had a cousin named John who told people about God's Son. John didn't live in the city, but he stayed in the wilderness. The people would come out of the city to hear John preach about the coming Savior.

John said, "God is sending His Son to save you from your sins. You must repent and stop doing wrong things!"

Many people who heard John repented and he baptized them in the Jordan River. Then they asked, "What should we do now?"

John told them, "Do things to show that you have repented. Help the poor and feed the hungry."

One day while John was preaching, Jesus came to the river. "Here comes the One I told you about—the Son of God!" John told the people.

"John, I want you to baptize me," Jesus said.

"No Lord, I should be baptized by You," answered John.

"John, we must do this to fulfill God's plan," insisted Jesus. So John and Jesus went down into the Jordan River. As soon as Jesus came out of the water, the heavens opened up. The Spirit of God came down like a dove and landed on Jesus. A voice from heaven said, "This is my Son, whom I love and am proud of," Jesus then began to teach others to love and follow God.

One day Jesus was standing by a lake where a large crowd was listening to Him talk about God. There were some fishermen nearby, washing their nets.

"Let me get into your boat," Jesus said.

Simon Peter, one of the fishermen, took Jesus out in his boat a little way from the shore. Jesus finished preaching to the people from the boat. Then he said, "Take the boat out into the deep waters and let down your nets."

"But Master," Simon answered, "We worked hard all night and never caught a single fish. But I will obey you." So Simon and his partners, James and John, let down their nets into the waters.

As they pulled up the net, there were so many fish that the net began to break. They filled two boats so full that they started to sink!

Simon fell on his face before Jesus, "Leave me, Lord! I am a wicked man!"

"There are enough fish here to make us wealthy men!" Simon's partners cried. "We will never have to work again."

Jesus said, "Don't be scared, Simon. God has a plan for you. From now on you will be fishers of men."

Simon Peter, James, and John rowed their boats to the shore. They left their nets and all the fish behind and followed Jesus. From now on they would help Jesus as He told others how to love God.

—*Taken from Matthew 3:1–17; Luke 5:1–11*

Think
ABOUT
—THIS

Why do you think God wanted Jesus to be baptized?

What did Jesus mean when He called Simon a "fisher of men?"

Setting the Scene

Read Matthew, Mark, Luke, and John to find out about all the places Jesus traveled during His life. Have fun making up several scenes to tell the story of His ministry.

John in the Wilderness

1 For the scene in the wilderness, cover some chairs with brown or gray sheets or blankets so they look like rocks. John can stand on the chairs and preach to the people.

2 Set up two chairs about four feet apart. Drape a blanket across the chairs. This will become the Jordan River, so blue or green works well. But since the Jordan was muddy, brown works too.

3 John and Jesus can stand behind the blanket so that it looks like they go down into the water to baptize Jesus.

Satan Tempts Jesus

After Jesus was baptized, something very important happened. Jesus spent some time in prayer and fasting to get ready for His ministry. During this time, Satan came to Jesus to tempt Him to dis-

obey God. Read Luke 4:1-13 to find out what happened. If you decide to put on a play of the baptism of Jesus, this is a good story to follow.

Fishermen on the Lake

1 If you decide to do a play about the fishermen, buy two identical nets. Fill one with cardboard fish.

2 Spread out a blanket on the floor to be the lake. Lay out the net with the fish on the blanket. Cover the net with a sheet or towel to hide it.

3 A large box, laundry basket, or wagon can be the boat. Or you can get creative and draw and cut out a boat from a large box.

4 Drop the empty net into the water and pull out the net with the fish.

FROM THE
Script

Go into all the world and preach the good news to all creation.

Mark 16:15

The Crucifixion and Resurrection

Casting Call This story has several roles that needed just the right people for the cast. First there was Pilate, a strong ruler who respected Jesus and didn't really want to kill Him. Then there was the Roman soldier who believed in Jesus as he watched Him die. Finally, Jesus' disciples who mourned deeply over His death but rejoiced at the news of His resurrection.

Wardrobe

Pilate: Basic tunic (see page 7), white sheet, gold belt, gold or green leaf garland, and twist ties.

Roman Soldier: Basic tunic (see page 7), cardboard fruit trays, string, scissors, felt, glue, silver spray paint, ribbon, and an old aluminum bowl.

Disciples and Mary Magdalene: Basic tunics (see page 7), shawl, head covering, bathrobe, and eyebrow pencil or face paint.

CAUTION

Have adult supervision when using spray paint.

Pilate

Pilate was a Roman ruler so he will dress in Roman clothing. Roman male citizens that were rulers or in good standing were allowed to wear a toga. Rulers of Rome wore head wreaths made out of laurel or bay leaves called "corona triumphalis."

1 Wear your basic tunic. If your tunic is not white, wrap a white sheet around your body so it looks like a toga.

2 Tie a gold belt or rope around your waist.

3 You can find leaf garland at a craft store. You can use green or gold. Twist it around several times to fit your head. Use twist ties to hold the strands together.

4 Roman men rulers didn't wear much jewelry, but a gold chain will work well.

Roman Soldier

Make a suit of armor using the following instructions.

1 Cut two single rows out of the fruit tray and spray paint them silver.

2 Punch holes on each side of the fruit tray rows. Tie a string through the holes. Then tie the fruit tray strips on your legs.

3 Spray paint two fruit trays silver.

4 Make straps to go over your shoulders our of felt strips 2 inches by 5 inches. Glue them to the top of the inside part of each painted tray.

5 Punch a hole half way down each side of the trays. Tie a ribbon in each hole and tie these at your sides.

6 Borrow a small aluminum bowl or pan from Mom for an helmet. Or spray paint an old sports helmet silver to look like armor.

Mary Magdalene and Disciples

Wear basic tunics, robes, shawls and head coverings. You can draw a beard with eyebrow pencil or face paint on the disciples.

Collecting Details

Who was released from prison so that Jesus would be crucified? *(Mark 15:15)*

What did Peter find in Jesus' empty tomb? *(Luke 24:12)*

Additional Props

● A scroll for Pilate to hold.
● Spear like the one on page 29 for the Roman soldier
● A shield like the one on page 29 or make one from a fruit tray spray painted silver.

Jesus Died for Our Sins

God had a special plan for Jesus. He had come to tell everyone about His Father. But some people hated Jesus. They didn't want to believe that He was God's Son. The teachers of the law wanted to obey God's rules by their own strength and power. They didn't want help from God's Son. So they had Jesus arrested and brought before the Roman governor, Pilate.

"So, is it true? Are You the King of the Jews?" asked Pilate.

"Yes, it is true," answered Jesus.

The chief priests and teachers of the law were angry. They accused Jesus of many things. They told lies about Him and tried to make Him answer their accusations. But Jesus remained silent.

"Aren't you going to answer in your own defense?" Pilate asked. He knew that Jesus had done nothing wrong. But Pilate had to keep the people happy. So he had his soldiers take Jesus to the cross to die.

Crowds of people watched as Jesus carried His cross through the city. "Crucify Him! Crucify Him!" They shouted.

His followers walked behind crying, sad that Jesus would soon die. They took Him to a hill called Golgotha, which means "The Place of the Skull."

The Roman soldiers drove nails in Jesus' hands and feet and hung Him on the cross. The people stood around and watched. They laughed and made fun of Him, "If you are really God's Son, save yourself and come down from there!"

Jesus could have saved Himself. He could have asked God to send angels to save Him. But He stayed on the cross. He died, because that was part of God's plan.

God wanted His Son Jesus to die for the sins of the world. Because Jesus obeyed, God will forgive the sins of everyone who believes in Jesus.

When Jesus died, the sky grew dark. One Roman soldier said, "He really was the Son of God."

Jesus' friends took Him off the cross and buried Him in a tomb. Because the Sabbath had started, they couldn't really prepare the body for burial. So three days later Mary Magdalene and some other women returned to the tomb to wash Jesus' body with spices. As they walked to the tomb they asked, "Who will move the stone from the tomb? It's too heavy for us."

When they arrived at the tomb, they saw that the stone had been rolled away. As they entered the tomb, they found Jesus' body gone. "Someone has stolen His body!" the women cried.

Then they saw two men dressed in bright white clothes standing near the tomb. They lit up the tomb like a bright light. The women became frightened. "Don't be afraid," one of the men said. "You are looking for Jesus, who was crucified. But I have good news! He is risen! You will not find Him here! Go tell Peter and the disciples. You will see Jesus later."

The women ran to tell Jesus' disciples what had happened. They didn't believe them and ran to see for themselves. On the way they met Jesus. "Greetings," He said. They were startled and amazed. "Do not be afraid. Go and tell my friends and brothers that I have risen from the dead."

This was all part of God's plan. Jesus, His Son, would come into the world, die, and then rise from the dead. Jesus did this so that we can become friends of God and share eternal life with Him.

—Taken from Mark 15:1–47; Matthew 28:1–10;
Luke 23:1–24:12

Think ABOUT THIS

Why did Jesus have to die?

What does His death mean for your life?

Setting the Scene

This story has several scenes. You can change sets between scenes to tell the story. Begin in Pilate's court then end near the tomb of Jesus.

Crucifixion

1 Draw and cut out a cross shape out of some large boxes. You can act out the scene of Jesus carrying His cross through Jerusalem.

2 Tape the cross up to a wall. (Ask a parent to make sure it's OK.)

3 Place a stool at the bottom of the cross.

4 Find an old block of wood and hammer. You can pretend to nail Jesus' hands and feet, by pounding on the wood. Be careful not to hurt yourself or anyone else.

5 Jesus can stand on the stool and spread his hands out to look like he is hanging on the cross.

Why did John outrun Peter when he went to Jesus' empty tomb? (John 20:4)

Because Peter had 1st and 2nd, and John had 1st, 2nd, and 3rd.

Pilate's Court

Set the courtroom up by covering a chair with a red or purple blanket or sheet. This is where Pilate will sit. A Roman soldier can stand next to him.

The Tomb

1 For the tomb, make a cave similar to the lion's den on page 39. In Bible times people were buried in small caves.

2 Cut a large rock shape out of poster board or cardboard. It may take several pieces taped together. Roll this stone in front of the cave.

More Ideas

● Have some kids dress up in white to become the angels who tell the women that Jesus is alive. See page 45. They do not necessarily have wings. Use small lights behind them to make them look bright.

● Make your story longer by having one kid pretend to be the disciple Thomas who doubted that Jesus was alive. Read about it in John 20:24-31.

FROM THE
Script

"He is not here; he has risen, just as he said."

Matthew 28:6a

More Ideas!

Look up these stories to learn great lessons. Use your imagination to think up costumes and stage props to act out the stories.

- Story of Faith: Abraham and Sarah—Genesis 12-21
- A Great Love Story: Isaac and Rebekah—Genesis 24
- Trickery and Deception: Jacob and Esau—Genesis 25:19-34; 27:1-45
- Loyalty and Friendship: Naomi, Ruth, and Boaz—The Book of Ruth
- Trust and Faithfulness: Shadrach, Meschach, and Abednego— Daniel 3
- Love for God's House: Boy Jesus in the Temple—Luke 2:41-52
- Trust in the Lord: Paul and Silas in Prison—Acts 16:16-40

Here are some more ideas for making costumes!

Crown

Make a crown out of a two-liter soda bottle. ASK AN ADULT TO HELP YOU WITH THE CUTTING.

1 Soak the bottle in warm water to remove the label. Draw a crown pattern on the bottle. The front will be higher than the back.

2 Cut off the top of the bottle around the crown pattern. Punch a hole at the base of the crown.

3 Fold down the crown and punch a hole through the base of the bottle. Put a paper fastener in the holes to hold the crown in place. The base of the bottle will stick up through the crown like a bubble-shaped hat.

4 Decorate with glitter and tie with elastic string to hold it to your head.

Cool Capes

- Pin two matching towels together. Then turn the hood inside out to hide the pins. Pin the front to keep it closed.
- Look for a solid colored shower curtain at the thrift store. String ribbon through the holes at the top. Throw it around your shoulders and gather it. Tie knots at each end to keep the ribbon in place. Now you have a long cape fit for any king or queen!

- Find an old skirt that Mom doesn't want or buy one at the thrift store. Cut one side of the skirt from one top to bottom. Cut a hole at each corner of the top. String a piece of ribbon through each hole and tie it in place. Now you have a great cape for a Roman soldier.

Great Things to Do with an Old T-shirt

- Stick your head and one arm through the head hole of a large T-shirt. Tie a belt around your waist. This would work for John the Baptist or Mordecai's clothes.
- Use a XXX large T-shirt. All you need is a brave strong grown-up. Put on the T-shirt. Put on the armor and helmet for the soldier. Climb on the grown-up's shoulders. Now you're ready to really play the part of Goliath the giant!
- An XX large white T-shirt makes a great angel costume. Dot it with glue and add gold glitter. Wrap a gold cord around your waist and you have heavenly attire.

Pharaoh's Crown

1 Wash an empty gallon size bleach or vinegar bottle. Cut off the bottom. ASK AN ADULT TO HELP YOU.

3 Spray paint the bottle gold. After it dries, decorate it with craft jewels.

4 Make several 3-inch vertical slits on the bottom of the bottle. ASK AN ADULT TO HELP YOU.

5 Put it on your head and adjust the slits so that as you press down slightly it stays on your head.

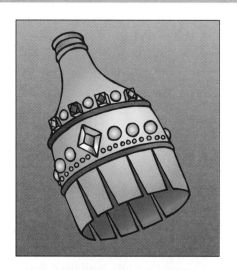

Clothed with Scripture

The Bible has some great things to say about clothing.

What kind of fur did Adam and Eve wear?

Bare-skin

Who made the first set of clothing?

Adam and Eve did! They sewed fig leaves together. (Genesis 3:7)

Did you know that God will make sure you have clothes?

"And why do you worry about clothes? See how the lilies of the field grow. They do not labor or spin. Yet I tell you that not even Solomon in all his splendor was dressed like one of these. If that is how God clothes the grass of the field, which is here today and tomorrow is thrown into the fire, will he not much more clothe you?"

Matthew 6:28–33

Who said he was not fit to carry the shoes of the Messiah?

John the Baptist (Matthew 3:11)

If someone takes your cloak, what else are you supposed to give him?

Your tunic. (Luke 6:29)

What did David say that God clothed him in?

Joy (Psalm 30:11)

What color robe did the soldiers put on Jesus before His crucifixion?

Purple (John 19:2)

Put on the Armor of God

Make armor by using ideas from this book. Mark each part of the armor according to the following scripture. Use your imagination to find ways to act out each part of the armor of God.

Therefore put on the full armor of God, so that when the day of evil comes, you may be able to stand your ground, and after you have done everything, to stand. Stand firm then, with the belt of truth buckled around your waist, with the breastplate of righteousness in place, and with your feet fitted with the readiness that comes from the gospel of peace. In addition to all this, take up the shield of faith, with which you can extinguish all the flaming arrows of the evil one. Take the helmet of salvation and the sword of the Spirit, which is the word of God.

—Ephesians 6:13–17

Get Ready, Set, Action!

Become a playwright and write your own plays.

You may have written stories before, but a play is a lot different than a story. A *story* has a narrator, description, and dialogue in quotes. A story is usually told in the past tense, present, or future. But a *script* for a play makes the events happen in the present. A *play* shows you what the characters are saying and doing. Telling about an event that happened is much different from seeing what happens to someone. A play tells the story through action. Bible stories are full of action and make great plays.

You can improvise, which is an acting term for performing without a script. Or you can write a script to tell the story. A script tells the reader about the characters and what they say, where the story takes place or setting, and the action of the story. If you decide to write a play you are called a *playwright*. The word "wright" means worker. So a playwright is someone who works a play, not just writes it.

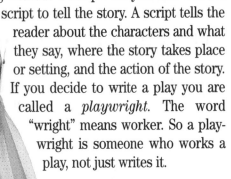

Here are some terms and tips for writing and performing your own Bible scripts:

● Every play needs a main issue or point. Scriptwriters call this a *premise*. For example, if you were writing a play for the story of Daniel in the Lions' Den, the main point would be that Daniel obeyed and trusted God no matter what. Think of what you want your audience to learn or be interested in as they watch your play.

● As you read the Bible stories, think of the action that happens. Picture in your mind all the exciting things that are going on in the story. How can you act that out in a play?

Backdrop

● Ask a clerk at a local furniture store to save large refrigerator or television boxes for you. You can cut these open and apart to make backdrops for the stage. Poster paint works well on cardboard.

● Paint the backdrop on white sheets. Latex or water based house paint works the best. Ask your neighbors and friends for half used cans of paint for a variety of colors.

● Use your imagination for special effects, such as a small fan for wind, rattling cookie sheets for thunder, or blocks of wood pounding together for horse hoofs.

● An old bedsheet, shower curtain, or blanket work great for a curtain. String a rope across the stage and hang the "curtain" with large safety pins or shower curtain hooks.

● The words spoken by the characters are called *lines*. The Bible doesn't always tell us what the characters said or thought. Think about the Bible characters. How can you show what they felt and went through? Then write lines for what you think they might have said in the story.

● In a play, the place where the story takes place is called the *scene*. As you write the play, you will have to write out the scenes, describing what they look like. Your stories may have several scenes. For instance, David and Goliath may have two scenes, the shepherd fields and the battlefield.

● You show the location of the scene using scenery. These are the pieces such as plants, tables, and chairs that create the scene. *Props* are the smaller parts of the set such as swords, spears, cups, and dishes. A *set* is the scenery and props created for the play.

● Every good play has a protagonist and an antagonist. The *protagonist* is the main character of the play and the one who gets things moving in the story. The *antagonist* is the character in the play that stands in the way of the main character's goals. For instance, in the story of David and Goliath, David is the protagonist. So who do you think is the antagonist?

● The *stage directions* are the playwrights' instructions for the actor, reader, and director about the scenery and the things that happen in the play. They are separated from the dialogue by parentheses.

Here is a sample of what part of the play of David and Goliath might look like written as a script.

Scene 2
(The battlefield in Judah. On the back wall there is a drawing of some mountains so that the scene takes place in a valley. A tent is set up on the right side of the stage.)

Goliath: *(Stands to the left of the stage and toward the back near the wall. He has his sword in one hand and a spear in another. Waving sword, he shouts and jeers toward the tent.)* Come out and fight me! Choose a man to come and fight me! If he can kill me then the Philistines will be your servants! I dare you Israelites to fight me!

David: *(Walks out of the tent with sling in hand. Slowly moves across stage toward Goliath.)* I'll fight you! How dare you test the Lord my God. *(David reaches down to pick up stones.)*

Goliath: *(Puts head back in laughter. And points toward David.)* Ha! You are just a boy. I will tear you apart and feed you to the birds. *(Points toward the sky.)*

Now you become the playwright and finish this play.

My Bible Dress-Up Book

Ages: 4-7 (I need help); 8-12 (Make it myself)

My child's need:
My child needs to learn that the Bible is filled with fun and exciting stories.

Biblical Value:
Faith

Learning Styles

Sight: Video tape your children as they practice and give their performances. Then some night, fix popcorn and watch the films together as a family. Children love to see themselves acting out stories. Talk to your children about how they felt portraying someone from the Bible. Does it feel strange to be someone you're not? What can we learn from portraying characters from the Bible?

Sound: Read Bible stories to your children and help them write plays of their own. If your children are too young to write, help them draw storyboards of the scenes in their plays. Listen to audio tapes of stories together to get ideas for new plays that your family can perform. Visit your local library or music department to see if you can find tapes of background sounds to add another dimension to your productions.

Touch: Create a fun activity of cleaning out your attic or closets to look for new props and costumes. Discuss with your children ways to bless people you know with the plays they have been working on (visit a nursing home or a shut-in member of your church, offer to put on a play for your Sunday school class, etc.). Practice, praise, and pray with your children about their productions.